WHAT ON EARTH IS A
meerkat

JENNY TESAR

A BLACKBIRCH PRESS BOOK

WOODBRIDGE, CONNECTICUT

Published by Blackbirch Press, Inc.
One Bradley Road, Suite 104
Woodbridge, CT 06525

Printed in Hong Kong

10 9 8 7 6 5 4 3 2 1

Photo Credits
Cover: ©Robert Cabello/Dallas Zoo.
Title page: ©Richard Kolar/Animals Animals.
Page 5: ©Ana Laura Gonzalez/Animals Animals; page 6: ©David MacDonald/Animals Animals; page 9: ©Anthony Bannister/Animals Animals; page 10: ©Betty K. Bruce/Animals Animals; page 12: ©David MacDonald/Animals Animals; page 13: ©Zig Leszczynski/Animals Animals; pages 14—15: ©David MacDonald/Animals Animals; page 16: ©David MacDonald/Animals Animals; pages 18—19: ©David MacDonald/Animals Animals; pages 20-21: ©David MacDonald/Animals Animals; page 23: ©E. Hanumantha Rao/Photo Researchers, Inc.; pages 24—25: ©David MacDonald/Animals Animals; page 27 (top): ©Gerard Lacz/Animals Animals; page 27 (bottom): ©David MacDonald/Animals Animals; pages 28—29: ©David MacDonald/Animals Animals.
Map by Blackbirch Graphics, Inc.

Library of Congress Cataloging-in-Publication Data
Tesar, Jenny E.
What on earth is a meerkat? / Jenny Tesar. — 1st ed.
    p.   cm. — (What on earth series)
    Includes bibliographical references (p.   ) and index.
    ISBN 1-56711-093-2   ISBN 1-56711-164-5 (pbk.)
    1. Meerkat—Juvenile literature.   [1. Meerkat.   2. Mongooses.]
I. Title. II. Series.
QL737.C235T47   1994
599.74'422—dc20   94-28250
                                                                    CIP
                                                                    AC

What does it look like?

Where does it live?

What does it eat?

How does it reproduce?

How does it survive?

TURN THESE PAGES AND FIND OUT!

A meerkat is a small animal with long, soft fur. Its tail is almost as long as its body. It has a small, pointed head, with big black eyes and a black nose. Its small ears are almost completely hidden by fur.

The meerkat's home is a burrow in the ground. Meerkats often sit or stand upright in front of their burrows. They like to sun themselves. But when a meerkat sees an enemy, it quickly pops back into its burrow.

A MEERKAT STANDS UPRIGHT
AS IT WATCHES OUT FOR
ENEMIES NEAR ITS BURROW.

MEERKATS BELONG TO A GROUP OF MAMMALS CALLED CARNIVORES.
MAMMALS FEED THEIR YOUNG WITH MILK. CARNIVORES HUNT AND
EAT MEAT.

Meerkats are mammals. Mammals are the only animals that have fur. They also are the only animals that have mammary glands. Mammary glands produce milk in female mammals. The females feed this milk to their babies.

One group of mammals are called mongooses. Meerkats are members of the mongoose family. Members of this family have long slender bodies and short legs. Most of them have long tails.

Members of the mongoose family are also carnivores. That is, they eat meat. They catch and eat other animals. Some of them also eat plants.

The word *meerkat* means "lake cat" in Afrikaans, a language spoken in South Africa. Meerkats aren't cats. And they do not live in lakes. But they do like water.

Another South African name for the meerkat is suricate. This word is also the basis of the meerkat's scientific name, *Suricata suricatta*.

MEERKATS GET THEIR NAME FROM A SOUTH AFRICAN WORD THAT MEANS "LAKE CAT."

EACH OF A MEERKAT'S FOUR FEET HAS FOUR SHARP AND POWERFUL CLAWS.

The average meerkat is about the size of a large squirrel. Its body is about 12 inches (30 centimeters) long, and its tail is about 8 inches (20 centimeters) long. On average, it weighs about 2 pounds (1 kilogram).

Each of a meerkat's four feet has four toes. The toes on the feet have long, powerful claws. A meerkat uses these claws to dig burrows in the dry, sandy soil of its habitat. It also uses its claws to clean its fur and its teeth.

Meerkats live in southern Africa, in dry grasslands and rocky areas. They live in groups called colonies. A colony usually consists of several sets of parents and their young children. Altogether, there may be 10 to 30 meerkats in one colony.

Meerkats live in burrows, which are homes built underground.

Each burrow has several tunnels and a grass-lined nest. Each burrow has several entrances, too. Meerkats spend nights in their burrows. Then they come out in early morning and warm up by sitting with their bellies turned toward the sun.

In the middle of the day, when it is very hot, meerkats rest in the shade of a bush or tree. Even when they hunt for food, meerkats do not travel very far from their burrows. At the end of the day, they curl up together and go to sleep in their burrows.

OPPOSITE: MEERKATS LIVE IN COLONIES THAT CONTAIN BETWEEN 10 AND 30 MEMBERS.
BELOW: MEERKATS DIG THEIR BURROWS IN THE DRY, ROCKY SOIL OF SOUTHERN AFRICA.

A MEERKAT FEEDS ON A GIANT CENTIPEDE. MEERKATS EAT MOSTLY SPIDERS, INSECTS, AND CENTIPEDES THAT THEY FIND IN THE DESERT-LIKE REGIONS OF THEIR HABITAT.

Meerkats eat mainly insects, spiders, and centipedes. They also catch lizards, small birds, rats, and mice. Sometimes they eat eggs, fruit, and roots.

Meerkats depend on their sense of smell to find food. They constantly sniff as they crawl along the ground and scratch in the soil. When a meerkat finds something good to eat, it picks it up with its paws. It holds the food in its paws as it eats—just like a squirrel holds a nut.

When it has finished eating, the meerkat sits back and takes another sunbath. Its front paws rest on its full belly.

The area where meerkats live contains many kinds of living things. There are grasses, bushes, insects, snakes, birds, and mammals of all sizes. Each member of the community is affected by things around it. For example, grass seeds are eaten by insects and small birds. These, in turn, are eaten by large birds and mammals, such as the meerkat. When the large animals die, they are eaten by tiny bacteria.

Many meerkats share their underground homes with other animals. Ground squirrels, mongooses, and small rodents often live in meerkat burrows. Sometimes unwelcome visitors, such as snakes, visit the burrows.

MEERKATS SHARE THEIR HABITAT WITH MANY OTHER KINDS OF ANIMALS. HERE, A MEERKAT CHASES A VENOMOUS YELLOW COBRA AWAY FROM ITS BURROW.

MEERKATS HAVE A NUMBER OF NATURAL ENEMIES, INCLUDING EAGLES, VULTURES, AND WEASEL-LIKE RATELS. HERE, A GROUP OF MEERKATS CHECKS THEIR SURROUNDINGS FOR POSSIBLE PREDATORS.

Some animals hunt and eat meerkats. Eagles and vultures fly through the sky, looking for meerkats they can eat. Large mammals, including jackals and servals, will often try to sneak up on meerkats as they sun themselves.

Ratels, which are members of the weasel family, dig into burrows looking for meerkats to eat. But if the meerkats are quick, they can escape through one of their home's many openings.

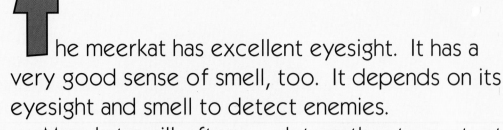

The meerkat has excellent eyesight. It has a very good sense of smell, too. It depends on its eyesight and smell to detect enemies.

Meerkats will often work together to protect themselves. As a group of meerkats hunts or rests, one member of the group stands guard. If the guard senses danger, it gives a loud bark or peep. All the meerkats quickly run for cover.

If there is no cover, the meerkats bunch together. They face the enemy together, as they growl and hiss. They move toward the intruder, jumping and screaming. This behavior usually scares the enemy and it runs off. The meerkats may then celebrate by hugging each other.

MEERKATS COOPERATE WITH ONE ANOTHER FOR PROTECTION. WHEN A GROUP HUNTS OR RESTS, ONE MEERKAT WILL STAND GUARD AND ALERT THE OTHERS OF POSSIBLE DANGER.

21

One of the most important activities in any animal's life is reproduction. Reproduction means "making more of the same." When meerkats reproduce, they create baby meerkats.

Reproduction requires a male meerkat and a female meerkat. The first step in the process of reproduction is mating. During mating, sex cells called sperm pass from the male into the female. The sperm join with, or fertilize, egg cells formed in the female's body. The fertilized eggs slowly develop into baby meerkats.

Meerkats mate about once a year. About 11 weeks after mating, the female gives birth.

A MALE AND FEMALE MEERKAT MATING.

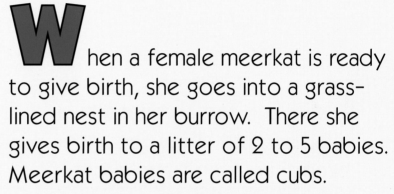

When a female meerkat is ready to give birth, she goes into a grass-lined nest in her burrow. There she gives birth to a litter of 2 to 5 babies. Meerkat babies are called cubs.

A meerkat cub is very tiny. It weighs about 2 ounces (28 grams) at birth. Its eyes are closed and it is completely helpless.

MEERKAT CUBS ARE TINY
AND HELPLESS AT BIRTH.

Mother and father meerkats are very good parents. They feed their cubs, keep them warm, and protect them from enemies.

At first, meerkat cubs feed on milk from their mother's mammary glands. When they are about 3 weeks old, their parents begin to bring them solid food. The cubs learn how to grab bits of food from their parents' mouths.

As they get older, the cubs leave the burrows. They go on hunting trips with other members of the colony. By watching older meerkats, they learn how to find food. By the time they are 6 months old, they are nearly full grown.

RIGHT: MEERKATS TAKE VERY GOOD CARE OF THEIR YOUNG. MOTHERS AND FATHERS FEED THEIR CUBS, PROTECT THEM, AND KEEP THEM WARM. BELOW: SOMETIMES EVEN OTHER MEMBERS OF A COLONY WILL "BABYSIT" A GROUP OF CUBS WHILE THE PARENTS GO OFF TO HUNT.

Meerkats are easy to tame. People in southern Africa often keep meerkats in their homes. They think that meerkats are nice pets. Meerkats are helpful, too. They kill mice and rats that live in people's homes.

Meerkats know that cooperation and working together helps them to protect their entire community. As they grow, they learn to look out for the fellow members of their colony. In this way, meerkats provide a nice example for humans to follow.

A LONE MEERKAT LOOKS OUT OVER THE FLAT, WIDE-OPEN PLAINS OF SOUTHERN AFRICA.

Glossary

burrow An underground home.

carnivores Mammals that eat meat.

colony A group of animals that lives together.

cooperation Working together.

fertilization The joining of a male sex cell, called a sperm, and a female sex cell, called an egg. Fertilization is a part of reproduction.

habitat Area in which an organism lives.

mammals Animals that have fur and mammary glands.

mammary glands Glands that produce milk in female mammals.

predator An animal that hunts other animals for food.

reproduction Making more creatures of the same kind.

scientific name A name for an organism that is the same everywhere in the world. It has two parts. The scientific name for meerkat is *Suricata suricatta*.

venomous Having glands that produce a poison, called venom.

Further Reading

Baker, Lucy. *Life in the Deserts*. New York: Watts, 1990.

Chinery, Michael. *Desert Animals*. New York: Random House, 1992.

Ganeri, Anita. *Small Mammals*. Chicago: Watts, 1993.

Gibson, Barbara, and Pinkney, Jerry. *Creatures of the Desert World*. Washington, D.C.: National Geographic, 1987.

Johnson, Jinny. *Desert Wildlife*. New York: Readers Digest, 1993.

Lambert, David. *The Golden Concise Encyclopedia of Mammals*. New York: Western, 1992.

Parsons, Alexandra. *Amazing Mammals*. New York: Random House, 1990.

Stewart, G. *In the Desert*. Vero Beach, FL: Rourke, 1989.

Tesar, Jenny. *Mammals*. Woodbridge, CT: Blackbirch Press, Inc., 1993.

The Sierra Club Book of Small Mammals. San Francisco: Sierra, 1993.

Twist, Clint. *Deserts*. New York: Macmillan, 1991.

Index